THIRSTY EARTH

Published by: The Atomic Underground
Website: www.TheAtomicUnderground.com
Cover Design by: Stephen Gros
Paperback ISBN: 978-1-954581-00-5
eBook ISBN: 978-1-954581-05-0
Library of Congress Control Number: 2021941566

THE ATOMIC UNDERGROUND

WWW.THEATOMICUNDERGROUND.COM

Keep checking back for new titles.

ALSO

We love our readers and welcome your feedback.

Let us know what you think.

theatomicunderground@gmail.com

AND

Like us on

Facebook

Twitter

and

Instagram

CHRIS WISE

PRESENTS

THIRSTY EARTH

THE ATOMIC UNDERGROUND
INDEPENDENT PUBLISHER
HOUSTON

DEDICATION

I dedicate this book to one of the great mentors of my life, Dr. Janis Haswell.

Jan, over twenty years ago, you read incarnations of some of these pieces. You attended my early readings where I blew boat horns in place of cursing when I was censored, and I threw wadded poems at the crowd. And yet, you still made me feel like I could write.

Your knowledge of W.B. Yeats and your dedication to the craft of writing have always amazed and inspired me. I will forever look up to you.

ACKNOWLEDGEMENTS

This work may have yellowed and curled, forgotten, unfinished in a filing cabinet if my friend, Kim Gentry, hadn't expressed such interest in me finishing it. So, here it is, Kim. I owe you a debt of gratitude for the long conversations, explorations, and motivation.

Thank you, Melissa Studdard, for your perspicuous line notes. Thank you, Winston Derden, for looking the collection over and offering ideas—as always, they were rock solid.

Also, here's a high-five to every ex-fiancée I've ever had for snapping my guts into scrap metal and dust. The pain kept me hungry and out of comfort. So, thank you for the art!

TABLE OF CONTENTS

INTRODUCTION

When I met Chris Wise twenty-four years ago, he lived in a rodent-infested trailer consisting of not much more than a place to sleep and a place to write. There was no food in the cabinets and only a can or two of beer in the fridge. His place was dark and smelled of wet towels. An old 12 dial television blared Dixie Chick's with what I would have sworn was "Ready to Run," although the song wasn't actually released for another few years. If I'd only known all that was to come, I may have never walked in. I might have run myself out the door like the scurrying rat that dipped out through a hole in the floor.

In many ways, the creation of *Thirsty Earth* is a documented journey of our friendship. Embarrassing in today's world but not uncommon back then, Chris and I started our friendship in an AOL chatroom on William Butler Yeats. Yeats brought together two people from opposite sides of the tracks, living in different states. With the kind of energy that comes from the young, we were high on Yeats, writing, and maybe some other things. I was a grad student working part-time in Kentucky, and he was a writer, tending bar in Lake Dallas. Life was his grad school, and in many ways, he was my professor. We'd spend hours typing or calling to share our thoughts on everything. If you ask, we could both pull out our "Chris box" and "Kim box," a time capsule treasure of printed communication, pages of writing discussions about our work and others. Many first drafts live amidst the hundreds in those stacks, as well as a phone bill neither one of us could pay. Kept over the years, we preserved this fleeting form of communication; maybe we were just vain enough to think it would mean something more one day.

Chris's distinctive gravelly voice (which he thinks came from nearly having his head cut off in an elevator accident) isn't my first memory. It isn't even his evil "I'm up to something grin" that has stayed with me. It's a green napkin. Not the restaurant, the conversation, the way he looked, just that he didn't know the color of a green napkin. It stayed with me; memories are weird like that. Perhaps it's because I already knew his love of Van Gogh's paintings and wondered for the first time what it must have been like to view the world through his lens. In hindsight, it's really kind of beautiful, but I was about to discover a lens I had never looked through.

Chris lived a colorful life, and I'm sure he has some recent kaleidoscopic stories to share. Back then, it was easy for him to keep much of his life from me since I wasn't living in close enough proximity to see it. Poems he had previously shared with me through emails and handwritten letters were a tough read. Why would a woman want to read about how a man thinks negatively about a woman's body and choices as he has sex with her? And if this poem was, in fact, reality as his collection's title *Real Time* suggests, what does it say about him and about what am I doing here? It's said writers should write about what they know best, and there were many of these poems in the collection *Real Time*. There are some gems in the pages and things I can later appreciate for the writer's craft, but there were those that made me--and still make me--uncomfortable. I wanted to believe the cringe-worthy stories and poems were simply a case of a writer's prerogative. Could the poems of women whose bodies offered too much or not enough be true? The booze, the anger, the waste, true? Sitting in that emotional and physical dark place, he cracked that dim door and allowed me in. Chris was indeed living a hard life. I was well-traveled and worldly; yet, still naive to the likes of Chris Wise. At an early Applebee's lunch, he confirmed these truths over a pitcher of beer. The sun hadn't been up long enough for me to indulge, so I watched him drink and listened to stories of wild happenings. My life was vanilla in comparison; most people's lives are vanilla in comparison. Later in life, with that jester-like grin, he'd say, "Kim, it's not that these lines are crass. Life is crass," and for him, life was.

In *Thirsty Earth*, a woven thread of mysticism brings a journey of insight to these harsh realities that isn't present in the collection *Real Time*.

Instead of the reader having to swallow a harsh pill, here narrator "Chris" swallows pills that are "tiny blue oceans of mercy," taking him to an ethereal place of escape and vision. Perhaps because *Thirsty Earth* is an esoteric quest to find absolution, the acrid truth is way more appealing to me, and maybe you, than the "crass" writing of *Real Time*. Here, the language echoes the time studying William Butler Yeats.

In writing this forward, I have struggled with the cyclical nature of our friendship and overlap to the creation of *Thirsty Earth*.

While I know this collection well and have been with it from the foundation to its final edits, introducing it has become a quagmire. Like the collection, our friendship has cycles where it would be put down for a while to be picked up a month, a year, sometimes too many years later. Often, it was these poems that would start our conversations all over again. Much like Yeats' gyre in *A Vision*, our friendship, and as a result, the collection would expand, narrow, and begin again; a yin and yang changing, moving as a living creation does. So too, Chris (the narrator) journeys through highs and lows, polarities represented between the narrator's pain and his escape through drugs.

Thirty Earth's orphic odyssey brings in strange characters and mystic drug-like revelations to the narrator, easing heartache only to grapple with reality again. Symbols such as cold and dark, compasses, and clocks offer the same dualities and spinning of direction and time as our friendship and the creation of the collection. There are deserts of pain and dreams of release. Occasionally, Yeats' symbols will appear in *Thirsty Earth* because whether in my Kentucky basement, his trailer, or sitting in his dumpster-found chair in Corpus, studying Yeats and writing poetry go hand in hand. Any good flea reveals its source. The moon, tower, roses, and such all found their way. While Yeats has faeries, Wise has dwarves. His nightmares about alien-like creatures, little blue men dancing made their way from an altered consciousness into the work as characters. Lizards and beings frolic like Yeats' faeries but in horrific form.

While Chris might tell you the editing phase was the least fun, it's where I see the most genius. What started as a boy's practice became a man's skill. The creatures became more complex, the quest more defined, and poetic license masterful. In revision, after feeling many of the poems read dull and not knowing how to fix them, he turned the pieces into prose paragraphs "in order to beat them up properly," offering himself fresh eyes to improve what he deemed terrible. The revamping took a beautiful turn with language now reminiscent of Coleridge through tongue-twisting ethereal images.

Thirsty Earth explores the deserts we all face: our thirst for more than the daily struggle, our thirst for the spiritual, and our thirst to quench the voices of longing.

If there is one thing I've learned from Wise through his life and collection, it is this: the journey is hard, but you keep on moving. If you find yourself ending where you began, this time, it's with lessons learned and a little bit of sleep.

Kim Gentry
Houston, TX 2021

PREFACE

To a Poet, who would have me Praise certain Bad Poets, Imitators
    of His and Mine

    YOU say, as I have often given tongue
    In praise of what another's said or sung,
    'Twere politic to do the like by these;
    But have you known a dog to praise his fleas?

                Responsibilities and Other Poems, W. B. Yeats (1916)

Elements within William Butler Yeats' poetry inspired this
collection, and I wrote it partly as an homage to him. This work's
roots draw from his poetry and his books, such as *Fairy Folk and
Tales of the Irish Peasantry* and *Celtic Twilight*, and explore themes of
religion, mythology, symbology, and mysticism, as well as love and
lost love.

What's fantasy herein will be obvious, but otherwise, the situations
and subjects I've addressed should ring true to life. I hope this work
is more pastiche than larceny, as I've tried to avoid being Yeats' flea.
But, if my readers say I've failed... well, then I suppose there are
certainly worse dogs on which to feed.

When light weeps,
the world shall end.

GUTTED FROM A LOVE GONE HATE

I called Brian to help
pass the long seconds
and endless hours.

"She only sees the bad," I said. "All laughs, all things we shared
forgotten or diminished by the pain.
She remembers how I told her never to say
she loved me
then asked to stick it—
well, it wasn't good; and that I said it in the same breath made it worse.

She can't forget the night I wanted to know if she was still on the pill
after I told her drunkenly that I wished she'd have caught me
with the hot Colombian stripper
in the bathroom at the party.

She remembers the late-night phone calls taken in another room,
the unfamiliar lace bra that turned up in the wash,
the outlandish stories to explain the lipstick on my belt.

She left me and is talking to someone better looking
in better shape who treats her better, and she won't come home
though I finally realized how I want to change
and love her,
even openly.

I'm on a heart-string leash
vulnerable for the first time in years,
and when I tell her my feelings, open up, she vents the rage.

It's like she hates me.
Brian, man, it's like she thinks I'm a bad person,
and all I want to do is change—show her I can be better,
that I can be a good man.

"Chris," he said, "we are bad people," and hung up.

I sat in the dial tone, alone, between the stark walls of my room

"So, it's true."

ALL DAY I IMAGINED CARESSING

The tiny blue tablets,
then swallowing them
with room-temperature tap water.

Without them, I'd have to think
of her—her photos, smile, the way she got excited
when she dyed her hair
or had her nails filled—everything
she thought I was ignoring.

She left to spend the weekend with a stranger
met through her internet ad.
She took nude pictures of herself so that he could see
made him short, sexy videos with the P.C. camera
I gave her for Christmas.

She spent hours looking at the photos he sent her in return.

If she flew back home tonight,
I would have known it failed, but she didn't.
She was having a good time.

I wrote my guts in a letter and taped it to her door
with a single rose in baby's breath,
and floppy, stuffed dog on the floor beneath it
sitting with paws out to greet what would never come back to me.

For the thirty minutes to her house from mine,
I prayed I'd see her car in the driveway
so we might talk.

I thought of the pills
for the thirty minutes back—tiny blue oceans of mercy
and drifting in perfect stillness with no wind,
silence and peace.

BLACKOUT DRIVE

I wouldn't say it was an overdose, but my breath hitched,
and I plummeted from my body.

The world gurgled down a neon whirlpool of greasepaint
until all mixed to black.

Lost.

Body dissolved, or abandoned, I drifted in the deep with no line
or point of reference.

The pills laid me low for sleep.
I convinced myself I'd grown tolerant.
The effects seemed long in setting and too soon leaving.
I was mistaken as I have often been.

Divided from my body, I could not find myself to wake
Time vanished. Place vanished.

I waited—silent, windless,
breathless, without even a metronome in my chest.

Then a star appeared
throwing hair-thin flairs
beckoning a vast distance above.

A single opalescent flagellum trailed thousands of miles behind me.
Reduced to a ribbon with consciousness, I began to move.

A baby's cries floated near,
and I drew myself closer to the light.

ARRIVAL

There were no bright angels or serpents
at first—
only a desire to travel through the starless heaven
towards the single point of light.

Excitement crackled through me
electricity, curiosity, instinct,
and then I heard the music!

Ancient instruments whirred,
drummed, chimed, vibrated, rejoiced.
The very air danced and sang!

The energy within me uncoiled in double helices
and my mind filled with poems that I did not
entirely understand.

I smelled smoke, felt needles.
My sinuses and tongue burned,
as I entered
the cryptic menagerie of the hookah!

DRUMMING PARADISO

From the pipe, the smoke addressed me
in the furtive phonology of the opiate.

Rarified, as its acrid tentacles, I listened,
tasting metal, listing,
while it mingled with my breath
and chanted of utopia.

> "With me listen to the dulcimer,
> the drum's measured beat,
> the chimes sing high and sweet.
>
> Bloom with poppies to paint the fields
> with milky bliss,
> hazy dreams!
> Watch worlds unfold
> to the unfettered mind.
>
> Follow me down the warren of corridors
> to watch the dwarves chiseling with their teeth
> at soft marble walls.
>
> Then inch with me, working shoulder and knee,
> through the tight spaces they carve.
> Together, we will emerge as oddities
> upon billowy, moss-covered rocks of the sacred valley
> where the sun always shines,
>
> falcons make their nests,
> and amid rubies
> roses grow."

But the couch, pitted and stained, stayed beneath me
while the valley sand swirled far away,
shifting, winding smoke-like
and undiscovered.

TOKENS

I awoke, lying in a desert lake.
Next to me lay two heavy, gold coins
ancient and hand-tooled.

I took them, bounced them in my hand for heft,
and held them out to sparkle.

On the head's side, the face,
minted in profile, riveted its eyes on me.
Then it grew and rose from the coin
ballooning like thin curtains in a wind I couldn't feel.

It turned to face me squarely, jaw hinging on pullies
in a clinch and yawn like a nutcracker.
The automaton spoke with a voice
accompanied by popping static as if played from an ancient reel,

> "Gaze into the ruby; God, blazes in a crystal, unconsumed by
>   fire.
> Listen to the sighing rose and smell the beauty of His word.
> If *huios* 'son' and *helios* 'sun' recall something from your norms
> search the raging sky and know you stand beneath Him.
> Then traverse this earth to suffer, accruing wisdom for your soul
>   becoming what you see,
> so know that one day you will sculpt yourself into
> a ruby of Heaven or a diamond of Hell.
> Beware the wisdom you seek."

The head lay back into the coin's relief and was silent.
So, I bit its edges to mark the authenticity,
and it bled in my pocket, melting
while I meddled forward, searching
for wisdom… or genius… or madness… or all three.

WHEEL ON

Blowing in a tumbleweed, a tiny chameleon
with telescoping eyes came to rest
on cactus spines near my foot.
Its strained voice floated up with dust
to weakly reach my ears:

> "People love to spin," he said. "It's nature. The galaxy spins
> pressing planets away from the sun.
>
> Time gyres like the helices of life.
> Rotating history moves 'round and 'round
> with slight evolution to each revolution of the passing wheel.
>
> Colors cartwheel from touchy-feely rainbows
> that grip the earth to stand amid evaporating,
> condensing, precipitating waters
> in their cycles.
>
> While men, drunk on life,
> find myriads of fascinations in this busy world.
>
> As their lives creep 'round, the sun climbs and drops.
> Calendars fall away. Memories are forgotten and made.
> Tornadoes screw down to make messes
>
> of happy, messy lives,
> all at the whim of the fickle wind.
> This dizzy world is mad, I tell you!
> But people love to spin."

So, I kicked him down the line
for the suddenly strong, strange wind to toss high
and pitch rolling him beyond the dune.
Then, I walked with no point of reference, fighting my natural line of
drift, my own personal Charybdis.

DIVINITY ALCHEMICA

Near a cactus summit reaching beyond mountain tops and stars
a hill of termites sat at services
looking conservative in dark Quaker dress—an elder preached his
sermon:

>"A transmutation has taken place," he began in a voice choked
>   with dust.
>"Something of alchemy! Still, we look to the heavens while we
>   pray. Do we not?
>Light is holy. God is still fire and pure! Is he not?
>Our savior from the endless night has assumed an avatar. Can
>   you hear me!
>
>From sun to Son, he has become! Has he not—has he not! I ask
>   you!
>His brow perdures, endures we are assured, insured, and we can
>   feel secured for sure!
>He will welcome us in the indoor, trapdoor, backdoor, front door
>   for the grand tour,
>and we will know him in all his gran-dure as his brow still shines
>   in brilliant gold!
>
>Can you hear me! Our art is still for him! Our songs, passion
>   thoughts,
>the way they've been since for-ev-er! But in the wind of alchemy,
>the artifices reflect modernity. Though at its core the celebration
>   is
>unchanged—I said un-chan-ge-d! and still, we are worshipers of
>   the sun!"

He raised his tiny arms, in the end, for emphasis,
and the congregation went wild
as he passed his hat for a second collection.

GNASHING SOLITUDE

An enormous green and brown leopard frog
in a blue, crushed-velvet top hat, sat with sad, downcast eyes,
his skin blistered by the desert heat.
He looked defeated.

A weak mind is contagious, so I went to pass him by
but was captivated by his soliloquy:

> "I've been sitting on this red sand mound
> quite a while... ever since I died.
> It's not what I expected.
>
> I taste burlap, and there are tares of many kinds,
> no flowers or green grass.
> I'm so thirsty, and there's no water.
>
> Occasionally, a hot breeze stirs the hot morning,
> or a cold one stirs the cold dark.
> There is no sun, only a glow that roasts the day,
>
> and at night, the starless empty heaven begs light
> from a broken, browned moon.
> I'm so thirsty."

His deep voice was a sad music.
He absently scratched at a blister on his leg.

> "There are no birds, rabbits in the bush,
> rainbows, streets of gold, St. Peter, or anyone to take my
>   account.
> There's no presence of God
>
> —only me
> and a weeping other
> I sometimes hear."

I noticed a walking cane of dark acacia wood,
collared and heeled with silver
laying half-obscured in the sand
at the foot of his dune.

Its handle was a sun carved of opal.
I took it up and returned it to him. The long edge
of his blistered mouth twitched, trying for a smile
it couldn't find, stirring a bottle fly.

The cane tumbled from his grasp again.
His choice made,
I pressed away from him,
searching.

SOMETHING BETTER

Peering through the fibers of this burlap bag,
I think I can see beneath the door.

There is a sunrise out there, something better.

I can hear the birds at their songs
caressed by the sun's first rays.

I can hear the traffic on the open road
and jets drawing lines across the sky.

I smell grass and hear the flies and mosquitoes
that want to touch me.

This tape that binds my wrist and ankles itches
and pulls tiny hairs. The rag in my mouth chokes me
when I try to swallow,

so I let it soak the saliva and blood. It's cooler that way
for the breeze cannot seem to find me.

… so hot and dark in here, but I swear
through the fibers of this burlap bag, I think I can see beneath the door.

There is a sunrise out there, something better.

HUM-DRUM DAILY LIVING

I awoke twisted and half convulsed
with my body shaking in time
with the ringing phone.
After a few misses, I answered.
A voice on the other end said:

> "You son-of-a... err... Mr. Wise, sir,
> you haven't paid your God da... err... bill
> in quite some time.
>
> We have been very patient,
> but it's up to 500 dollars now."

Through a yawn of what felt like
my first breath all day,
I said, "I'll get my checkbook," and tossed the phone aside,
while I clumsily struggled to untangle the rope of sheets
from my tingling limbs.

I did that every time,
and I never looked for a checkbook.
Instead, I went to the cupboard—empty
but for one old can of navy beans
that I'd held out on.

Then I opened the fridge
for a can of Extra Gold,
an off-brand beer
worse than widower's piss
on a sale that was hard to pass.

Had a drink,
winced and peeked
out the window to my truck.
The windshield crack refracted like a blinding laser of sun.
A new windshield cost 500 bucks. Who had 500 bucks?

Three knocks erupted at the door.
I checked the peephole.
The property manager saw me peeping
as she posted
another eviction notice. Rent was 500 bucks.

With eyes too heavy to raise, I turned up the radio.

It said war still loomed.
A desert country had again vowed
to avenge revenges
revenged upon them
from their original revenge.

I undressed to shower, stopped by the scale,
still too fat
from too much Ramen and Hamberger Helper with no meat.
Tried to suck it in—
no change.

Defeated, I went about my standard routine of doing nothing.

One day, maybe I'd pull the money together to please them all
but not today.
Instead, a bitterness fell over me
like I needed revenge for trespasses
I could barely remember.

I felt angry at the whole system and resolved to reject it for as long as I
could.

With a discount beer and a dollar-store can of navy beans for provisions,
I settled in to wage a personal war of protest
or for a vision quest,
while the phone rang clogged with calls
that I couldn't afford to answer.

WHAT SHE TOLD ME

Sitting on the floor, working a jigsaw puzzle,
pushing beer cans away to find stray pieces,
I remember old conversations from before she left.

"I don't know if you're lonely," she began,
"or if you don't know how not to be alone.
You'll probably die a lonesome old man with a lot of books.

It's how you treat people.
You don't let them in
and keep a distance.

You say one thing like, "I don't want a relationship."
Then you do another like flirt and mess around.
You're a hard read,

a very complicated man.
People mistake that for your being a bastard,
and they leave.

Maybe you're all busted up inside or something,
but people get hurt,
and you can't go around doing that... breaking hearts."

After she left, I went to my room, alone, and took up a book.
It's what I always did.
It was all I seemed to have,

but then I got this puzzle,
lost her,
and I've been picking up pieces ever since.

REASON AND REASONS

I sat by candlelight contemplating suicide
one cold January night,
thinking nothing made sense anymore.

All my dreams screamed like kettles
evaporating steam
in darkness

the night Joy crowded its belongings
into my ragged, burlap suitcase
and hopped a plane for the West Coast.

I ran my longest ring fingernail down the middle of my chest
past the bellybutton and up again in repetitions—
made a red line.

I imagined being split supine on the autopsy table
by bored doctors who search my withered liver with a dipper
for evidence of foul play.

The candles burned low.
One candle my father made—a cocktail of wax and wick
in a martini glass that reminded me to drink,

but all my bottles and flasks lay scattered and empty.
The other candle ran like regret
all over the floor.

I didn't know what to think anymore,
but these days and nights had to stop.
Living like a wraith, I missed work.

People were starting to talk.
They said I lost the luck I used to know.
Maybe so...

Joy wouldn't come home for me, and to hang hope that it might
only made life worse. I had to find relief or die.
I felt angry that I had no easy answers.

I got up, showered, blew out the candles,
and ran out with no money
and no coat.

MY CELESTIAL SHE

The moon watched. She watched it all and didn't say a word.
She was there when I took the twenty-fifth line from the strange coffee table
and licked clean the bitter credit card.

Paling a bit, she watched,
and I could see she wore another scar.

She stayed with me, though, outside the window
when I bought another and another fix.
She watched me through the restless fits.

She plunged no arrows in my heart to punish, neither end nor start
of another night's debauchery.

Never revealing my misdeeds, she kept my secret safe
shrouded in the hearts of her and me.
She is always there to see, always there to witness me.

When times she speaks through the soft voice of my inner-mind,
she warns me to safety, but I don't listen or hear her well.

So far away is heaven high; her voice rings faintly in my stubborn mind.
This does not dissuade her, though, not even in the least,
but I can see she wanes a bit when I fade south from east.

Brightly lit among the stars, I can see the blemish of scars
that she displays proudly for me. She makes herself a beacon of sheer tenacity.

When it seems I am lost, she is there and will not leave.
Virgin Huntress watches all and shares the pain with me.
Each time I digress from my charade of desert purity

and leave the sand for rail and train
I hear her weeping
faintly within my mind.

Then I watch another scar appear, self-ashamed and teary-eyed,
as she pales a bit, wincing from the pain.

9:59 A.M.

Wind songs strong against the windowpane
rouse me too early
with nothing to say.

Varying intensities
stir densities
of particles, birdsongs, and applauding leaves.

Thin clouds whisper secrets
sneaking across the sky,
and the sun is a hologram with no heat.

This morning's jukebox-conspiracy
of procrastinated responsibility
drones on the strings of my conscience,

out of tune and time,
old melodies that
I have learned to ignore.

NO COMPASS OR CLOCK

Lost in the wasteland of addiction,
I circled in eddies of a whiskey monsoon
then dried out, belly up
on the sands near thorny underbrush.

In the beginning, the circle spun lazily.
Fields of life lay
damp with optimism and clean with rain,
but the spiral tightened as I cycled closer to bedrock.

Choked by drought, the fertile turned fatal.
Landscapes faded to a hellish tan of whipping sands,
and I was caught somewhere between dust to dust and the moments
before.

Demoralized, feeling I had traveled too far to be nowhere,
it seemed hopeless. With no plan and low spirits,
I resolved to die in the rough sands of the desert.

Dizzy, I sat upon a dune and prayed for a sparkle of mercy
in this thirsty abyss of wind-blunted stone and heat.
Then waited and waited, longer still.

ALPHA DAY RUNNING

I melted on a red sand mound
like a candle burnt to grease.
Traces of sulfur spoiled the wind.
The bitter taste of pills sizzled acrid on my tongue.

Crushed beneath swelling lamentations
I couldn't rise.
Visions of regret threaded in like bare-pated vultures
crowding at a corpse while I gazed up from the dune.

I lay beneath a sky of technicolor galaxy patterns,
feeling shattered and scattered in geometric repetitions
dwelling on redundant contemplations
of could-a should-a, and her.

I dragged together like mercury finding itself
to walk and search for the virtues I'd once so naturally possessed,
and resolved if anyone would help,
I, at least, would listen.

ONE COLD TURKEY DAY

My body ached as if the blood had pooled and clotted.
Electric light from the window said the sun had set.
Minutes passed, and a tingling dotted and sparkled
through my cold feet and cold hands.

My groggy pulse stirred like consciousness from a coma.
Uncertain how long I'd lain,
I looked at the clock.
It flashed, shocked by a power outage.

I wanted a turkey sandwich, felt thirsty, and wanted sex
or at least new love and a tomato,
and to clean up from drink and drugs and reform
and to eat a bag of pork rinds.

I heard detox brought demons, but what the hell.

THOSE OF THEY

Groggy, slit-eye stoned, or sober
I see shadow beasts with yellowed, switchblade teeth
hover over my shoulder.

Roaches and rats dart around corners,
animating every shadow
until finally, I chased—

then, the apparitions distorted,
raced at me,
tentacles and tails collapsed together into solid shapes

with maws agape
inches from my face, the red, yawning canyons
screamed baritones too deep to hear,

only felt
quavering through the marrow of my flexing bones.
Malicious, they roar from throat and groan through grease-black darkness
until, at last, invoking as huge, grotesque heads on little bodies
or swirling bone dragons of smoke.

Smaller legions are also there.
They stand one-half and four foot in numberless ranks beside the others
crowding too tightly, far beyond the dirty room we share, staring,

deathly silent, perfect in rigid formation
travelers from a land of shadows and half-dreams.
They watch.

At breakfast, I wonder over cold oatmeal and withered berries
honeyed with old crystals from the lid
if they come from the Spiritus Mundi,
if they are horsemen behind Ben Bulben's white triangle.

"Where are you from?" I howl. "Say! Say!"
The drain pipes gurgled and hissed, "Thhhhheeeeeeeeeyyyy."
Small and lonely in the emptiness, I waited

for something more than panic,
more than horror,
Something attacked, possibly, a rat in the attic—a thrashing,
then stillness.

NO WESTMINSTER MELODY

I dropped the weights and brass hammers of excess today
inviting in sunshine's golden pendulum
through Venetian slats of self-abusive trends.

The blinds bent shadow bands over the pallid husk of my body
like prison stripes caging a mind
worried with fortune's and tragedy's tock-tick-tock indifference.

For my own good, I confined myself to seclusion
though I preferred the base dreams of dust, and smoke,
and strange women, and books—
even risking company with "Those of They."

Though I claim that I'm back
to replace the pills, beer, hard habits, and all things
that scar with purer aims

the tick-tock of seconds splitting mahogany
ring the timepiece in my chest
and shatter rare wood chips beneath the pendulous ax

of the great floor clock
until the pitiless pendulum sways,
and I escape into the wilds,
rushing back to madness, dogged by the pops of busting springs.

THROUGH THE SHEE

In the mock-death of sleep, I've breached Sorun Jive,
a place no one goes but the impish lords of its moors and plains,
for there dwell a people called "They"
who ride war-painted ponies with flowered manes.

I've seen them dancing; I've heard them sing;
I've watched them with their changelings,
spied their wiles at berry vats,
caught them torture water rats.

Some know them as Pooka, "good folk," Fae, or Wee
others call them "horsemen," fairies, or the gentry
euphemistically,
but their name will always be "They" for me.

They've stalked me through my waking dreams
raced nightmares out to punish me. They've sought to drive me mad
for what I know—for what I've seen.
Their almond eyes, hard and dark chrome-green,

seize pleasure
in the endless menacing.

WICKED JESTER

The gentry who, when time began,
were maggots feasting through the rocky skin
of Ymir, the venom-born giant of stone and frost,
often gather close to hear my autobiography of dust.

In what they claim is a just exchange, they gift me
draughts of cold, Urdarian water for discourse
and mad dances with my sapient soul.

Their water sets my eyes towards geometric heaven
where gods of all nations walk in rows of perfect sevens
whispering, in rhyme, the wisdom of forever.
This trade is dangerous, though. They feed a little
on the soul—nostalgic for the days of old

when they were carefree larvae chiseling labyrinths winding and low
tasting metals, ice, and stone. Incorporeal, yet more than shades
these good folk they call "They" make formations of incalculable ranks
and long to hear me speak. They seldom issue a weak reply
standing mute with eyes unblinking dark and watching. Their flesh is
tanless as the grub.

> "Beware the Jester," they implore. "He assumes enchanting
> forms which are said to hypnotize through costume and illusion,
> but you may know him by his eyes with the strictest attention.
> Avoid his savage appetite, for he is not mosquito light.
> His wild cravings are so bestial they consume."

Consulting their astrology, their shamans urge me to mind my memory
and obtain the mystery I've searched for in our visiting
else their legends say he will kill me
while I dream.

TAPESTRY OF HEADS

A tapestry of severed heads,
bound with hairs of golden thread,
carols for rhythm while I sleep.

Twisted and bruised with bloat and rot,
noses withered, eyes in knots,
they keep the beat for nightmares that plague
my writhing slumber.

Naked heels on crushed stained glass
dance it down to blood and sand
while lizards—the sun's most holy followers—
bob their heads and sing of Armageddon.

In each of their pockets
burn rubies:
reminders of God's red fire.

But I am a beggar with no precious stones
left alone to wander the wastelands,
a pauper with only echoes in my out-turned pockets—
the echoes of hands and fists striking, stainless blades shining,
distant voices crying, and music from a carousel.

This evil preys upon me in my deep repose,
choking me until I finally explode from a dream,
knotted in sheets, gasping to horsely scream
through the tumult of the loveless night:
"Why does a moment of happiness cost so much sorrow?"

THE EXCLUSIVE CLUB OF THE SUNRISE

I hear working people rev cold engines
so heaters warm when the sun rises or moments before—

a comfort to prelude discomforts
of their employment.

Pulling a blanket over my head, I grumble something
about how they should quit, blow their money

on women and beer, move into a trailer bedroom
to shiver in the leaky window wind until they pass out—
be happy as me.

The sun rises for them, offering a welcome to the day
with all of its safe beauties as I drift off
from the dangerous unbecomings of the night

scorched to char by chaos engines
and my bitter unemployment.

Let them have their heat.

ICE SHEPHERD

My breath's gray fog floats
past frost-bitten starlight
shimmering through my ice-candied window.

Under several blankets, I try luring the Sand Man
from his beach house to spirit me to sleep now

by counting sheep, but the flock fades butchered,
tumbling past the ceiling fan's frozen blades

in a splash of chill wool congealed into ice crystals
shaved and heaped in dirty snow
over and through the chattering springs of my mattress.

THE LONG HOUR

I sat in the long hour, again confused,
naked on the edge of the unmade bed,
unsure if I wanted to shower or go back to sleep.

This place, this prison, this crypt
rotted my disposition. I had no T.V., money, or gas;
I wanted out but had no place to go,

no friends to call, only her.
I tried reading *Mrs. Dalloway*
but felt too much like Septimus,
couldn't focus. I had dishes and laundry to do
but felt like a roach—heart crushed by a nightmare boot.

The phone rang. Too eager for contact,
I didn't check caller I.D.
It was her.

In case I'd forgotten: I was still a cheating, lying, lazy,
drunken, no-good-son-of-a-bitch.
She was still a brow-beating, harping, unforgiving,
unrelenting nag, with an impossibly selective memory.

Her dying phone put us out of our misery.
No healed feelings would come of the call.
No forgiveness or reunion,
but it did chip me off the sty of sorrow's eye.

I decided to shower, yes, a shower—
Something to wash her voice from my ear
and a gargle to rinse the wrath
I choked back.

LOW AS HIGH CAN BE

I tasted something bitter in the sugar cube.
I had powers to see bluebonnets budding,
red clovers cloving, sunflowers sunning,
iris blossoms dilating, daffodils disgorging
dark blood high into the bright shining spring afternoon
with each pulse from the breast of Mother Earth
on a green hillside in a damp pallet of color.

I cooled in the fine crimson mist—everything dotted
and mottled by its deep blush. Tiny dwarves burrowed up
like earthworms to chatter and kept me from sleep,
but I traded a rhyme for silence, and they left me
to all of my addictions,
visions, and thoughts.

Back on the wagon, I ignored good sense from dwarves
and everyone. Half dead and stretched over my sweat-wet bed,
I dreamt of dramatic plans
to cloak the truth, so well,
I'd hide it from even myself.

THE LED AND THE NOT

"In the beginning, there were similes and symbols."

The clear words fell like fog around me
and sounded as if I had spoken them myself,
but I smoked from the spine of a great cactus hookah
feeling sorry, maligned, and drowsy.

"What?" I asked.

A lizard with knowing eyes climbed around the cactus spike,
up the scorched edge of a desert rock, and explained,

>"A train barrels through the desert,
>cleaving blue sky with charcoal black,
>led by its engine, led by the track.
>It is society.
>
>Passengers in its chambered cars perceive luxuries.
>They trade ideas, lace fingers, play poker, exalt the wicked.
>All gamble and win less than the lizard."

"Of course," I said, pretending to listen.

He continued, "Hooded hawks circle, haunting the train—
>lost spirits eternally wait for it to lead them to a home
>where the train never goes.
>
>Lizards sun disinterested in the sand
>with spiny backs and rough-beaded skin;
>they forsake the train's luxuries to follow only their basic needs,
>ever free, each one basking in the light of heaven."

The lizard paused dramatically, awaiting my comment
on libertinism verse stoicism or some such,
but he caught me zoned out.

"Did you say something?" I asked and coughed a little.
Then my eyes rolled back into the tracks of my skull,
and I smoked on like Johnny Cash's Old 97
charging up the Danville line—

wherever that was.

THE SPIRITUAL PERDURE

In this arid land of golden tan,
I braced against the whipping sands
and turned inward,
recalling what I'd read
on the faded parchment scroll
I found hidden in the hollow
of a sun-bleached camel bone.

"Lizards—speckled black and yellow—sit puffed chest,
back arched to soak the harsh
life-giving sun.

From clarity, they occasionally recall
why they fled the train—

lies, political zealots, prisons, killer children,
greedy evangelist, and the entirety of Creation
leaning ill.

At night, lizards dream of light and shroud themselves
in the camouflage of warm, safe sands
that retain the day's passion
until they emerge to stand
conspicuous and confident in the morning.

And, when subtle things conspire to hunt
them for sustenance, testing them in seasons
when the sun feels too distant, they bury themselves deep
meditate and sleep, dreaming of the time to emerge
and rediscover the lost light."

Wind blew the parchment,
down the distance
over dune and ditch
for other travelers to decrypt.

I muddle beneath the moon,
unsheltered through the darkness
with no coat, or money, white-knuckle dreaming
hoping for a little light and heat.

THE CANYON

Didgeridoo words echo through
these canyons.
Baritones sang by Gentry float from where
a mirage of Mab, the Fairy Queen, bathes
beneath crystalline waterfalls carving scars
through the dusty cliffs.

Her shower songs remind me that
tomorrow echoes today, and we live forever caught
within the defiles of our canyon,
our mortal life, and eventually our grave—

while around us, flowers swim on tides of wind
with hummingbirds. Purples and reds quiver and somersault
through golden pollen, and nectar swells
through prisms of golden light
and light showers.

She invites my melodic reply. It fails.
I return a life of wrong answers with years lived unmoved
until she beckons me to chase.
I have caught her on rare occasions,
and the fairy queen offers "pleasure or money."
I keep only echoes in the chasm of my sobbing wallet.

I have taken pleasure every time.

FORBIDDEN PRAYER

She fades away, shriveled, skeletal,
stripped to the molted
pill-blue capsule-like carapaces
of insects sliding, crisp, pitched
across the craggy embankments
of yesterday.

Moments before, we'd lunched
in the Desert of Longing at the ruins
of an oasis on cold fruit plates
beneath palm shade
wearing streaming linen shirts,
beside a flowing basin,
commenting that the patterned tiles
of the toppled mosaics were well-painted, well-masoned.

An arrangement of shofar blows rose over the ruins
from the canyon below—
echos of a prayer whispered long ago
that lifted then fell like a reaping blade.
Many times it rang, disturbing everything away at breadth
because, once in haste, I breathed
what none should ever say: "Lord, give me what I deserve!"

She disintegrated in the twisting sand.
A thorn pressed sharply into my palm
where once I'd held her hand.

Alone, ashamed, I crumpled on the dune
with nothing left but ragged breaths
and a conscience stained with blame.

IN THE PAINTED DESERT.

In a crumbled adobe stall, I saw
wedges and squiggled latrinalia carved and painted
on an ancient bathroom wall
in what I'd guessed to be a woman's hand—
a bathroom poem for oblivion.
Luckily, I had the Rosetta Stone app
on my cellular phone
to translate the cuneiform.

It read: "Desert hills roll out in blue horizons and thorny shrubs.
     The dry mid-afternoon air is bleached bone still.
     These crystal skies have not seen rain in 298 days.
     A great horned toad sits
     in the shadow of a stone
     curiously watching a hawk,
     dizzy in its lazy circles.

     As the two make eye contact, the toad stoically lifts his right-
          front leg
     and flips out his longest middle finger.
     The hawk cuts the silence with its shrill scream
     and paints him with white, hot shit.

     In the deserts without man, it was business as usual."

Less poetic than she,
with a shard of tile, I added to the graffiti,
"I was here, wish you were too."

Then I drifted out to chase mirages of toads and hawks and lost love.

MIRAGE

She weaves in gypsy robes of sinuous blue and gold
shimmering with the desert heat.

Streamers of floating gossamer spun
by Athena's spiders lifting out in billowed sheets.

I search for her, this belly dancing henna princess soft as dew in sandaled
feet.
She is a mint-laced whisper weightless as her fabric's vapor sheer

never drifting near
ever rocking out of reach.

LECTURE OF SOUL

I awoke with my soul in a cockroach.
It stood like Father Time on a bag of rice
in a cabinet over the oven.

He wore a monocle on a gold chain and spoke eloquently
with excellent manners, aside from the fact,
he was stealing my rice.

He cleared his throat
and said,

> "Refine your philosophy, defy temptation.
> Indulge in thought and constructive recreation.
> Leave emotion to the ocean tempest, swallowed without line,
> without direction until you fish from the brine a beauty perfect
> for planting your affections. Then, quell the swells and strive.
> Strive for strength together. Fight at length to love her.
> Love her forever and know life
> from the death you had before!"

With a napkin, I crushed him
in a fist, lightning fast! He never had a chance
because I didn't want him to.

He was a thief. I stole back my soul and rice, despite his rhyming advice
then flushed him where all thieves belong,
considering his words while he twisted down the pipe.

DROUGHT

For miles, nobody stirs but the luckless.
Books have no flavor today.
Bills belch over in tall, unpaid stacks.
Wallet empty, payday, and employment—a desperate wait away.

Wasted time sings in second-hand pipe chimes
outside the window.
My guitar leans out of tune.
Hardcore movies lay in unwatched heaps.

Across the room, I see my figure distorted
on the surface of a brass doorknob.
The knob won't turn or latch or reflect as well
as yesterday's bitter stainless-steel lament.

My memories with her—all straight razors and scrap iron.
I felt so cool telling her, "the grass elsewhere will be greener."
I've walked bald deserts ever since.
Tonight, I'll pass among the luckless

looking for a plot of healthy sod and take my place
among the ranks of those who held happiness, here, in the palm
to let it slip like sand through careless hands while the chimes
outside play never-ending songs of accidental music.

THE COLD AND THE CALLOUSED

She finalizes paternity papers
with her ex-fiancé tomorrow evening.
I called to say how I wished I could be there
to support her, kissing her ass good,
trying to win her back,
and swearing I was a new man.

"I don't know what to say when you tell me that stuff, Chris."
I asked, "You think it's a load of shit?"
"Maybe not, but it smells like it."

I threw my head back and laughed,
thought she was joking.
She wasn't.

"It's just not you," she said.
"So, who I am is not supportive?"
I felt crushed.

Every day, she opened my eyes wider to see
the no-good-son-of-a-bitch people said I was.
What everyone whispered was true.

"Yeah. You aren't supportive," she said, then had to go
leaving me uninvited and unwelcome.
But before she hung up, she told me not to drink myself into oblivion,

but I never listen to her.

SHELTER

Today, I heard a young and pretty woman shading beneath a sun umbrella
    complain
she's led a sheltered life. She wanted to see the world.
"Merry-go-rounds to porch swings," she said. "What happens to us along
    the way?"

I wish I'd known her well enough to say, "There is nothing wrong with
    shelter.
The world can be a maelstrom of painful, ugly things. With age comes
    focus.
Focus isn't as fun or reckless as we'd like, but it's efficient, healthy.

Porch swings have that easy glide with only a soft push of the legs.
Merry-go-rounds are faster, but too much work and leave you dizzy, out
    of focus.
When the sun and sky are this bright, when hummingbirds are dancing,
    and the breeze is right,

do not complain that the world has not been harsh enough to you. How
many days of rain before another one like this? Who will complain about
shelter then?" But I said nothing, shrugged, and we watched her children
play from the shade of her sugar-white umbrella.

A MOMENT OF PEACE

When I lie down after mixing pills and whisky,
acid burns in my throat, making it hard to sleep.
So, with eyes closed, I remember moments from years past,
recreate a smile, smell, conversation.

I see grandmother's kitchen, her small wood table,
the centerpiece of plastic grapes, a pear, red apple.
They were hollow and never dusty.

I remember afternoons in a pecan tree,
looking out over the busy street,
watching automobiles crash at the intersection,

or when the Doberman jumped from an old Chevy, dangling
from its harness-leash until the driver helped it—
yelping in terror—back into the bed.

I remember a girl I loved,
holding her while she slept and laughing.
We laughed a lot before the end.

On rare times, I run in a big yard playing
in the evening light with old dogs I've had—different ones
that were stolen, lost, killed, or distempered.

I wonder if they wait in heaven with my grandparents
or if there is a heaven. I imagine all I could meet if I make it there.
Then finally, memories mingle with the pills
and the whisky, the acid, and the dreams.

THE PIT.

I never mind warning labels. I do what I want.
Pills helped me dream—the liquor was a habit.
But my legs disagreed,
and my head smacked the coffee table corner,
then the hardwood floor.

A spider from beneath the couch, brown and thin, walked to me,
legs moving like fingers on piano keys.
It stroked my ear and whispered,

> "Down the corridor of ancient stone
> past shadows where the tortured groan
> lies the pit.
>
> Opposite the tunnel,
> love and light await abysmal sights
> after razor, pills, rope, or shot,
> then a drone and a cold wind.
>
> They plummet through a well
> of grasping hands that clutch,
> strain, claw to touch
> the fallen's new skin
> then harden,
> crack and crumble,
> into striking serpents
> with painful poison
> before splashing in the shallows
> of desolation.
>
> Creatures of supernal creation
> rush in mobs to touch
> what they wish so much
> they were.
>
> With receding gums and flesh of slime,
> these abominations of earlier times
> exist to take some to the pit.
>
> They escort souls by torchlight
> down a passage

to a gate. Some turn back,
some boldly wait
but opens soon the iron grate.

A moment passes,
the escort moves on,
stirring the dust of those long gone.
They take souls to the pit.

Arthritic hands
with vice-like grips force them
to look within
though the things themselves
avert their filmy eyes.

From the waters of the pit, visions appear—
children unborn, families torn
all that was had and to be received.

Yet tales remain that the greatest pain
shows across the faces
of the gazeless things.

They despise those in their grip
for the ungrateful, shortsighted lives wasted.

Still, they release them to a second chance
at achievement, happiness, love, and bliss.
While they themselves endure lessons
and in darkness perdure.

Heed their warnings.
Beware the fate
of Hell contained within the gate.
Live lessons of your holy writ
and praise the blessing of the pit!"

The spider crept back beneath the couch
to the chords of its web.
I did not like his rhyme. Being a slow learner,
I merely dragged myself to bed
resting in the pit of my buckled mattress,
believing I'd had enough
of bugs.

THE HALLS OF LEER
(A Province in Hell I Have Found)

After many campfires in the Valley of Low,
I ascended the far wall of Forlorn Canyon.
At the escapement's crest, I came to a fork in the road:
one well worn, the other less traveled.

I started down the less traveled road.
It ended in a grotto guarded by a flaming skull
that came to attention and spoke
through a quivering jaw,

> "Abound in darkened halls of Leer
> lurk phantoms, dragons, and visions clear.
>
> Dungeons cold with dank and stench
> boast strong iron chains and well-masoned brick.
>
> No guards, no crowd, no prisoners remain
> only echoes of terror, ax scars, and stains.
>
> If ever you find that you're in the caverns of Leer
> by dream, or by drug, or meditative sphere,
>
> escape right away and never return
> lest your soul become branded and doomed to burn
>
> then added to the chorus, added to the screams
> married to the dungeon and tortured by these things!"

If it said more, I'd never know.
I found the fork to the road more traveled
and raced quickly down it,

learning less traveled roads
often lead to places
no one should or wants to go.

THE WATCHMAN

On a frosted peak of jagged rock
in a range called Heart, on a holy spot,
I met The Watchman, a hermit
whose sun-blasted face and gray eyes
stripped me to the soul.

He lit a dark, well-crafted oriental pipe
and watched me for an age unmoving. Silent.
I could smell the brine upon him and knew
that he had come through the abyss.

I waited in the smoky haze,
apprehensive, listening for what he had to say.

"Can you hear the choir?" he said at last.
"The choir of spirits your organic body has dressed and left
decomposing then recomposing
time after time and time again.

The dust of dust is a choir singing its wisdom
all the time, for all time.
Your thoughts echo this. The ideas you call great
are all born of this. One day, you again will sing with them
sooner than you think."

He cleared his throat and nodded towards a small table.
I set the white envelope with his fee of thirty-six fifty on it.
He puffed his pipe,
cracked ten fortune cookies,
lay the messages in a stack,
closed his eyes, and continued.

"This is your poem which I prophesied:
Ancient mountains fall.
Elders die burdens, outcasts.
We lose importance.

Limbs bare. Hearts fade gray
humanity at winter
Divorce soul. Flesh. Mind.

A banshee has come
painted on thin clouds above.
Fear the siren's call.

The crow caws to earth.
Butterflies dance on the wind.
One day, your spring comes."

He puffed his pipe a little more and continued his report.

"In every clime, find
that flowers of all seasons
will blossom for you.

Let the world crumble.
Eyes find beauty through the heart.
Chasm take the rest.

Beware the chasm.
You are closer than you think.
Resist its allure.

Treasures are questions.
It's the journey to answers,
not answers themselves.

Quest beyond the flesh.
Find your riches in wisdom.
It crushes nightmares.

I walk nightmare's neck!
I am one with forever.
Listen when dust sings!"

I began to hear the choir too. Was it genuine,
or had the smoke of his pipe
affected me? I began to eat the fortune cookies.

"They call," he said, rising to leave.

As if to share a secret, he turned back,
then thinking better of it,
quit the idea,
and was gone.

I sat on the mountain alone—crunching
intermittently
on the cookies.
A cold wind fell over me,
and it settled itself around.

STAGGER TRACKS

I'd thought it was a pill, crawling
by a bend of iron track.

An Ox beetle tumbled down a face
of crusted sand struggled forward,

so exhausted it could not stand.
I used my toe to flip it upright
off its opalescent back.

"I have traversed the Desert of Addiction," it said,
"with nothing in mind but a drink.
I have crawled up from the Desert of Distress,
too blinded to find mercy in the sun.

With envy, I have seen others in the periphery
who never even noticed me
while basking on Sands of Felicity.

We have impatiently
stood next to one another at the grocery lane,
traffic light, veterinarian's office.
Yet, our deserts differ vastly.

Though happy, they seem bored with its drought
of daily repetition.
My deserts seem to burn much hotter
with longer days and less shade,

but we all thirst. And there is no atlas for our wastelands
of ever-changing shifting sands
that never end."

"The luckless and the lucky," I said, "stagger together
from one mirage to another in all their varied deserts
trying to dodge the blistering truth."

Its horned head nodded. "Drive on," it said,
and our tracks fell behind in winding divergence.

ONE PURE TRUTH

I sat near the skeleton of a burned-out motorcycle.
The sun was furious. Even cirrus clouds had hidden
from the two o'clock sky.

I wore a wide-brimmed straw hat
and wrote on a scrap
of wood shingle.

A large desert crow strutted over
and asked me for a smoke, then a light,
then to borrow my hat.

I accommodated him; then, he ridiculed me
for scribbling in such scorching heat.
I told him, "What I write won't lie.
It won't flake out or take advantage.

It doesn't ask a thing of me
that would further transmute
this hardened heart to jade.

It offers only the miracle of self.
With this pen, I can drop my guard,
choke up whatever ails me,
be human—things I can never do in person."

The bird began to laugh.
He leaned my hat fashionably to the side,
and commented that it was easier to be a crow.

Then, I spat on him and walked off.
Some people you just can't talk to,
and they wouldn't get it if you could

UNBEFITTING SACRIFICE

The tumblebug lay on his back,
arched with limited movement
until his legs finally slowed to stop.

It pitched one-quarter way round,
bridging, yet unable
to right itself.

After a night of network news,
riots, bombings, police brutality,
brutality against police,
and so many half-truths that it couldn't sort them out,
it lost the will to live.

After checking its Facebook page,
finding all the political arguments, photos of greasy meals,
and invitations to play some kind of game,
he'd suffered what turned out to be apoplexy
within the exoskeleton.

With no hope for the world
and no longer feeling able to stand the other insects
of his social circle, he saw no reason
to call for help
or make any last requests

before the step
of the sympathetic
boot.

BEATLEZEBUB

I woke to it eating on my shoulder.
Long, thin, armored legs
scuttled between my sheets
between my body and pillow.

I sat up, startled, groggy.
My sleep-clouded brain calculating
the mathematics of fear;
my arm darted, as if by instinct,
through the blackness.

I snatched it up between thumb and forefinger.
My slow mind puzzling, processing, feeling.
Strong, thin legs spread wide and swam the air,
a stony body—the carapace of a hideous beetle!

My heart kicked. I barked like a crow
and threw it to the ground.
In a flash, I launched out of bed to turn on the light,
my brain calculating the mathematics of attack.

Like a rainforest devil,
the spiked and thorny bug charged me
from under the bed, mandibles wide
and ready to feed.

I fell upon it, hammering with my fist.
A puss of guts burst from its side, but it would not die.

Thinking quickly, my brain calculating
the mathematics of defense;
I pulled a toothpaste box from the trash to trap it,
but first, I found a pencil and stabbed it,
then tried to crush its head off.

The pencil snapped, and the bug still would not die.
I scooped it into the toothpaste box
and left it there, scratching and rasping at the inside,
all day—the cardboard prison of its death.

Later, after it finally died, I snuck a look
into the well of the box. A gold-type beetle,
serrated mandibles, six legs or so—
something out of Hell hiding in chaos to gnaw me.

So, as much as I hated to do it, I cleaned;
if cleanliness is godliness, for now,
this house is hallowed ground.

THE MISERABLE VOID

I erased her messages just now,
saved from before we split,
when her voice still held something for me,
old messages

because for the longest now,
she's had no time for messages,
no time to call.

She said she would talk with a girl
she suspects I cheated with.
I never did but saying so wasn't good enough.

Today, we had planned to grab a beer after work;
I changed my mind.
They were talking in her office when I walked up.

She didn't know I could hear through the door.
"He can try," she said about us, "but it's not going to happen.
There's nothing there."

I made my shoes quiet on the high-gloss floor
and walked away.
And now, staring off into the blueberry midnight
from the window of an IHOP,

I try to remember what life was like
before the chaos,
but nothing comes to mind.

HAIR TRIGGER

No matter how much I wash,
I still find her hair curling off laundry.

Before, I'd smile, take it delicately between two fingers
and let it float to the carpet that I rarely vacuumed.

But then she left me for another cock who uses her
as her emotional hazards demand.

I rip away the hairs now, snarl, and mock
how they are different at the roots.

I fling them down like pestilence
and curse her out loud

though she isn't present to hear,
and I still rarely vacuum.

DAEDALUS NEAR

I turned the room over, looking for pills.
I needed a lift
but crashed on the runway.

I heard great wings, smelt an early morning rain.
I dreamed of Daedalus rowing through the sky
with mechanical wings painted in sun and silhouette.

Daedalus spoke from a rainbow near:

> "If you dream of flying away, gather wisdom.
> Leave all that work against you,
> escape!
>
> The small thinker imposes false sanctions over you.
> With a skilled mind, set yourself apart,
> soar free with unfettered thought.
>
> Be warned—fly too close to the sun and boil in zeal
> like my Icarus,
> and if too near the brine, death waits in the shadows and cold.
>
> But, if you tap a fine line of travel
> between the zealot and the godless,
> you may soar with me balanced and free
> on your own wings among the heavens and the promises."

I wasn't sure I understood.
My body ached.
I lay in a fever, tasting salt.

DREAMING OF ELYSIUM

I reclined on a truck-bed blanket,
waiting in solitude while waves rolled in.
Numberless and thin, clouds boiled smoke signals
past the moon—a cross-hatched message
from the future—offering precarious reassurance.

Herrings hunt in haunted shadows of shallows, trumpeting
like Furies in Tartarus.
No stars rippled the black heaven.

Instead, I saw all my nights in hooker hotels, hungry and hung
on my last chance. I remember bats chattering in the flickering
streetlamps
and black poplars rooted in the city.

The gulls laughed in trash-barrel flocks—billy goats like me.
Nomads.
Nothings on a beach of nothing.

I looked up at the cold, grey moon
pocked from taking shots since it was born.
"I can take it, too," I howled. "Life ain't whipped me!"

I listened to the clouds. Silence.
The miserly boatman would have to wait.
I had no coins left.

In the black distance, I heard the echo of his horn.

BEACHED

I washed up in the rough surf of tangled sheets
sometime after 10:30
in waves of cold.

Death-breath busted,
the space heater sat in gray enameled
silence.

Marooned, I lay on the queen-size wasteland
watching the dog pace
like something from the fathoms—hungry and expectant.

Bottles lay spilled on the nightstand.
Empty. Inside there was no message,
no remembrance, no love returned,

only the cold emptiness of this room,
and possibly, if I listened closely,
the ocean's song.

THE EYES

I thought it another nightmare, but it was madness.
I know that now. I awoke startled with something wrong—
a pressure constricting my groin.

Clicking on the table lamp, I stripped away the covers
and my garment.
Horrified, I found 32 eyes the size of buckshot

burrowed and nested around the base of my cock, darting
frantically in all directions,
periodically blinking, looking for a point of focus.

I pinched them, but they would not pop,
then I clawed them bloody. They would not focus.
Panicked, I slid out the blade of a knife

I'd been sharpening day and night
from its leather scabbard—a 5 ½" razor
that shaved hair in a single pass.

Poised to slash, I grabbed the shaft
of my penis and pulled it straight.
The eyes widened in shock,
looking for something to save them.

I let the blade sink in an inch from the base
and skinned off the top plate of flesh,
then went to work on the sides.

I cut them out each one,
each of all the blinking eyes.
The pain was incredible,
but they had to come out!

I cut for 20 minutes until I could find no more,
could take no more.
The blur of madness begun to fade.

"The Eyes!" I screamed. "Where are they?"
I searched the scraps of flesh. I smeared through the tacky blood.
The knife fell when sanity took my legs out.

Together we lay spilled over the ground.
Blood wrecked and blind.

THE CITADEL OF MADNESS

A buckeye butterfly flexed her wings high
upon the spiny side
of an ocotillo cactus.

All the eyes of her wings watched.
I trudged beneath her, lost
wishing I'd an atlas.

"I can't take much more of this," I said.
"This place is driving me mad."
The eyes upon its back spun like slot machines
and coins freezing on sevens and tails.

It spoke: "Within the Citadel of Madness, genius is held.
        Years it takes to scale its wall and map a path
        through its labyrinth of halls.

        Still, if ever the dungeon is beaten,
        the cunning one who perseveres
        will emerge into the foyer of paradise

        where genius sits half entrenched in its ruby throne
        awaiting embrace. When cautiously wrestled
        from its resting place, behold a breath of roses,
        and the key to unlocking the deepest wisdom
        shall be at hand, But beware!

        That wicked subtle serpent who at the beginning
        sowed the tare is waiting to catch a cunning seeker
        with the key brushing at his fingers while he springs

        his well-played trap, so that sanity snaps to crash
        for all the world to witness their brilliant minds fade
        away and dull as they are doomed

        to forever dwell locked in that citadel
        called Madness."

"Exactly," I said. "Though I have no audience,
I wilt bloody and ignored in the lunacy
of rusting anonymity."

ABOARD THE WHEEL

In the dark emptiness of safety,
my hedgehog runs on his wheel.
His work is his hobby; his hobby is his job;
his job is to run all night.

Round and round: Squeak, squeak, squeak, squeak.
I listen at the deadbolt locked in paranoia.
The house smells like lemon Pledge,
but it's cluttered with coins spilled with crumbs
through the cushions of the second-hand couch.

Limping around the house because
I'd cut myself, believing that the bleeding
may be cleansing, but it wasn't. Everything's a mess!

The trashcan mocks my art.
It says I've smoked the tires of life for nothing!
No love. No friends. And my books—like all the books
of most dead poets—will only rest woven
through the mess of the landfill

swallowed like the trash of flesh I wear—a casket
for everything in its time.
I shrug and tell the trash, "Everyone knows it's all for nothing,"
but we look for comfort where we can,

even if we're a simple hedgehog running on a noisy wheel,
even if we all sometimes
go a bit mad.

THE BECKONING

Purple, floral curling smoke
wraps the air with incense like a key
cast by a shade smith
to unlock blueprints beyond.

I inhale my capacity
and slip into trance.
I am seated upon a great, hot ruby;

tubes pierce my forearms
running through
a colossal copper
alchemical still.

A Bible stands curled, crushed
into the alembic,
but no roses pour from its pages.

The gold of transmutational purity
will not find its way to my veins.
The ruby flashes
and I am blinded.

The book has disappeared.
Eros, his veil rippling with laughter,
ridicules that I will not
give in to his greeting,
pursuing Dionysus instead.

He mocks that I am

"the fruit of a fallen tree
full of seed,
futilely planted
on a rock."

Then, disappointed, he leaves,
saying that I

"have much to learn.
Ideas and doctrines are nothing
without practice."

The air clears.
I half expect to find the lacquer
of some floating formaldehyde beast
draining its way to my veins
or a pickled, crippled fetus
in the beaker,
but the lamp and receiver

are also gone,
so left upon the massive ruby,
I gaze at the fire trapped inside
its crystalline walls and wonder

at the scars where the tubes were
in my arms
given by those folk of shade
who name
and proclaim
me Enigma.

WISHING WELL IDOLS

I tracked the slide of a sailing stone
to a trophy-sized
rose rock.

A dove cooling and cooing
in the shadow of a nearby outcrop
said,

"We are two symbols of love here,
the rock and I,
and maybe we're both bogus."

Its feathers fluffed
as it gave itself gooseflesh
with a squish of urohydrosis.

"It's hopeless here," I said. "Why have you come?"
Twisting its head far to the side,
the bird painted the lower ledge white

and spoke:
>"Tokens of hope, wishes, and fancy
>mark the well with copper and silver disks down dancing
>through rippled waters deep.
>
>Idols on the bottom collect hope and coins
>indifferent to the symbols that they'll spend.
>When through the quivering wave, a wisher watching sees
>
>spinning and dropping tokens fall too close
>to the grasping hands of their hero idol,
>and truth to them is known!
>
>Magic gone, idols crumble,
>hope still lost, wisher humbled
>realizes there is no marble man or hero perfect,
>
>only disguised gods—frauds,
>thieves of hope
>and coins.

Eyes wide, the wisher see the stone cherubim
pissing a fountain in their well of hopes.
Realizing what water his heroes swim,

the wisher moves on,
broken
to find another well

while idols exposed,
recompose, and wait
for another wisher.

I have come
to warn
you."

The rose rock began to crumble.
I thought the bird might startle
and fly up,

but its head twisted
the whole way around,
and it crumbled, too.

Together they fell like coins
cast down into an ancient
and forgotten well.

THE WELL AT AUVERS

Never safe in a dream
while the soul vaults in quest
delving into worlds beyond the realm of consciousness.

I've been in the church at Auvers
and seen in its basement bones,
especially by the well.

There, from the darkness, I heard the drone
of the troglodyte's lonesome baritone
and grew ill from a carrion smell.

So terrible my tremble, I tensed and nearly woke
but relaxed at just the moment
before the vision broke.

I sunk into the well past much slimy brick.
The walls clenched about me
till I reeled near faint and sick.

The cavern at the bottom was a den of puddled ponds
where a shabby heatless lantern flickered poor illumination
on infant bones like cobblestones and his draconian mutation.

Shattered idols strew the floor weakly reconstructing,
then crumbling, crashing down once more
believers numbered few and poor too weak to keep them standing.

Near a corner crystal pool, the lizard man knelt weeping.
His ruby eyes scorched rippled water
across the darkness gleaming

while he droned a prayer tripping weakly from his lips,
murmuring through echoes in cadence with the drips
falling like full tears from high since the last of the last apostles died.

> "Here though shadows scarcely move, they're pregnant with their
>   secrets too.
> Sorrowful Mothers, their fresh-born rained to this stony floor
> female babes who'd never sing knotted with their birthing
> chords.

This well has hushed the suicide falling from the top
and from the stealthy murderers caught their silent crop.

Clumsy drunks and hopeless brides gazing from the rim
have met the ancient, crumbled idols
who have waved them in.

I have known them all
tender soul to busted bone the last to lick their worried
ears with my whispered baritone."

I stumbled back half-drugged to clear my foggy mind.
His change of tone brought welling fear
the fire left his ruby eyes. He dropped his thin veneer.

A hive of roaches stormed the sides spinning through a smoke
          of flies
that choked up with the sulfur
stinging sharply in my shielded eyes.

He lurched wild for my throat, his face a foul contort
an umbilical that tied his navel to the cavern floor
sung out like fired bow and stopped him dreadful short.

In sheets, twisted, wide awake
tethered to my bed,
the comfort of the crunching mattress quickly cleared my head.

Vanished was the vastness
of the black and murky cave—
the grotto of the troglodyte and its many secret graves.

My Van Gogh framed in plastic cracked and fell from the nail
the traveler, reversed in graphics,
walked the other trail.

How like the lizard his disguise!
How lit with fire his diamond eyes!
I had met the evil one in gestation as he spawns.

Already he has taken lives spanning ages all.
I have seen the first to come
when Armageddon calls.

MAGIC IN BETWEEN

I snagged in a field of thistles half-dead
amid the prickly blue and purple blooms.

Caterpillars, the size of donkeys,
chewed milky leaves
and spun me round with silk.

They admeasured strong tobacco
that nearly stoned me comatose.

I should have felt afraid
that they could be carnivorous
and bellicose, but they sang

softly in whispers
while they worked:

> "Dance with us on the middle ground—
> the beach, the dusk, the dawn
> to watch the magic happening here.
>
> Lean with us upon the ancient trees
> arching at the darkened wood's periphery.
>
> With us taste the grassy plane
> rocking to its lessons on the harmony it sustains,
> before we emerge as oddities to drink the nectarous wind."

I felt myself change, splitting in the chrysalis.
I saw a crack of light and felt the warm wind.

I grew stronger and then fell.
Panicked, I began to
flex and float

until I joined a rushing storm of moths
frantic for the here-and-there of flame.

INVOKE

Young daemons dance in the fire.
I hear their song that floats along
with popping wood and sizzling sap.

Moths hear too, and hypnotized draw near
to find death in the daemons' trap.

I stoke the fire with green wood,
inhaling the heavy smoke
considering headlines of note—

the decay of cultures, species' numbers, and the world.
I listen as the little daemons joke
and dance the wood to ash.

REVENANT

Blistered in the harsh desert heat,
I fell into a hollow
parched and ready to die.

A cactus pad with iron tines
laid its gentle shadow over me,

bejeweled with flowers of strawberry-red
that turned and spread their voices
in C minor like a tabernacle choir
doing their best to lift me.

      "Soak the ruby's rapture and be free.
      Become the falcon, fowl of the heavens,
      vaulting beyond the trees

      Awaken with the brilliant morning, ever free.
      Cast sleep from the tired eye of the higher mind.
      Ride the thermoclines steep.

      Or be the iron tine in trying times.
      When the world trips on the spikes of your grit;
      teach it the weight of gravity.

      Join us ever free above the common consciousness,
      where sorrow is a haunt and cannot dwell,
      where ecstasy finds no parallel. Awake and see!"

I resurrected from that shallow sand grave,
stood, and kept moving
refreshed and optimistic.

My muscles felt stiff,
but I was a miracle
Or maybe masochistic.

RISEN

Termites in dark Quaker dress
led me twenty-feet down a great many winding steps
into the labyrinthine mound to a sweat lodge

dedicated to the burning of spearmint incense
near their baptismal jacuzzi of tea tree
beneath the desert sands.

Naked, we meditated, breathing sweet leaves,
letting impurities
transude,

waiting in the interlude beneath a chrome red light.
Dripping condensation shed
the rough-shod tribulations

of life puddling around us
until our consciences lightened
and our consciousness loosed.

I conquered visions of the screaming locomotive,
as it hauled society down the long grade,
along the switchbacks,

transporting billions of intransigents in car-after-car stacked
and filled with their sour crude and corrosive selves
steadfast and full of bombast down its hell-bound track

while Hercuxar, the termites' strongest woman
fed the cauldron
hot stones.

Then, they rubbed spearmint oil, shining, onto my skin,
healing all ravages of the sun from without and within.
My spirit rejoiced as it fled the rails,

unafraid at last, lifting on a thermocline
until resting in a desert lake, finally at zero
with nothing between the sun and me.

Even if to a few termites, my tale was merely another testimony
for them to witness and holler "Hallelujah!"
and tattoo the drums with water weeds.

A LOCUST SINGS OF ARMAGEDDON

A locust sang from a camel skull
in a balding vest of camel hair;
a lone voice raised in the wilderness
warned this world is threadbare.

Knowing predators lurked around us
and that all the world calls his race a plague,
it quaked, afraid, yet sang on anyway!
I rested near it, by dry bones,

dust-covered in the valley low
listening to the raspy tones
of everything it had to say
in the strange, symbolic hymn it sang:

> "Lift your hearts
> let the piper strike a tune.
> It's winter in the churchyard,
> and the tower's falling soon!
>
> Pillars ring its girth,
> stacking high its many floors
> towards nothing.
> Now the tower leans, profaned.
>
> Meant as the moral center, gleaming clemency built for man,
> but its foundation strained from all the trains
> passing through its base and built upon the sands
> that now gather close and high to topple it at last!
>
> Lift your hearts.
> Let the piper strike a tune.
> It's winter in the churchyard,
> and the tower's falling soon!
>
> For long ages, lizards loved its marble purity
> and strong columns—a thing of God it was!
> But gold crept into beauty. Diamonds flashed about,
> and the smoke of trains dark-grayed the marble white without.

The sun blazed its rage;
the atmosphere gave way.
This day's been long in coming.
Paradise is drumming on the wind!

Lift your hearts.
Let the piper strike a tune.
It's winter in the churchyard,
and the tower's falling soon!

The desert sands consume again,
blasting through judgment's wind
to bleach the tower and howl amen
before it brings it down.

Impervious, lizards rejoice
and rise to two legs, happy
in the doom of doom.
Rapturous, their chorus booms.

Lift your hearts.
Let the piper strike a tune.
It's winter in the churchyard,
and the tower's falling soon!"

AFTER FORTY CENTURIES

The valley stretched into a plane where grasses spoke
in whispers born of a god's breath.
The dancing blades said that the time is near.

Civility diminished, fear has wound fetters tight
across the tongue.

Rage boils hardly concealed
beneath the surface.
Life is cheap, and purity is a joke.

Aries appeared in a field of bluebonnets,
as a pale translucence in the light of the waxing gibbous moon

looking vexed, waiting for another yet to come.
Dumbstruck, I dropped the mushroom caps I'd found to eat
and could not speak.

Neither fairies nor crickets sang aloud;
only grass had cause to sound.

Shadows shifted, and I stood alone.
The flowered dew-damp glade empty and silent
except for a single firefly ascending high in groggy spirals

like Hades disguised as a bit of fire, late
having overslept a reunion planned after forty centuries of emptiness.

The Apocalypse would have to wait.

I NEVER SPOKE TO ATLAS

At zero in the frankincense,
I move stoic past fallen pillars
that pock white and gray the glade
where the Titans died.

Then fades sun and shine,
sound of surf, and smell of brine.
I'm overtaken, spirited away
by an all-consuming fog.

There is woeful singing in the air.
I know the words from another dream
though unwilling, I too begin to sing,
feeling this other's despair.

Suddenly, I find myself in the abyss
stepping on stars to make my way.
I see Atlas, the source of the singing,
kneeling and leaning, the world low on his back, stretching high.

Before I ask, he reads my mind
and says he weeps for what he must do.
The world, he goes on to say, has fallen to decay
the way it always does when it slips low upon his back.

Soon again, he must juggle it up
for a better grip and seat upon his shoulders.
The earth will shake when its great plates slip
and tear her rocky hide.

The molten tides will flow and rip
and scorch the earth alive
This is why he weeps; he says
This is why he weeps.

I formulate another question,
but he knows the answer still before I speak.
Civilizations will fall away, he says.
Many will be lost to time,

but some will be found again one day,
and just enough of the ancient's ways
will remain to be baffled by their wit.
Atlas lowers his head, beginning his dirge again.
When I decided to sit and wait,
sing with the god, and avoid this fate,
I was retaken by the fog and returned
to the scent of frankincense

where I half-dreaming heard sirens
race by in the night
and the crash of neighbors
brawling next door.

A FULL EIGHT HOURS

I came in from working late
and checked the caller I.D.
Nothing.

She hadn't phoned.
But the desperate panic of heartache had dulled,
and I finally felt life without her.

Back to myself like I used to be:
lonely, surly,
drunk, and mean

with lessons from the Hard Way
on devotion, loyalty,
other people's feelings.

I learned better what love is and how to handle it.
I readied for bed and stretched in the light of the unlucky moon
who knows nothing of romance.

Maybe I'd rounded as a human being
becoming more vulnerable,
even a little gentle,

because after many near misses and lucky escapes
feeling the punch of being crushed.
Then, for the first time in months,

without the aid of pills
or hours of staring at the comatose phone,
I drifted into a dreamless sleep.

APPENDIX: THE MENAGERIE

Symbols and dreams, with the right juxtapositions, bring nuance, weight, and flavor. But, as T.S. Elliot discovered with the *Wastelands*, they can also lose readers. If the poems are too abstract, readers feel annoyed and dissatisfied. For example, Ezra Pound's *Cantos* are so densely loaded that I often lose the poetry. It's so full of histories, art, self-indulgence, economics, etc. that he even called his book a bit of a "ragbag." So, aside from feeling impressed by him, on an objective level, I rarely choose his work to read.

My readers can feel relieved to know two things:

1. I did not just compare myself to Elliot and Pound because that's silly as hell. I'm only stating that I do not want my readers lost on my poetry like I can become lost on the poetry of Elliot and Pound.
2. The notes that I offer below are neither the last word on all I intended with these symbols nor are they accurate for every instance they appear in the collection; this is only the best I could explain them during this sitting. It felt important that I at least attempt an explanation, even a thin one before the book goes to publication (and thank God, after over twenty years of working at it, it's on its way).

Acacia wood – This represents immortality, renewal, and purity. It was used to build the Ark of the Covenant. It is also a psychoactive plant and is a source of DMT.

Alchemy – The mysterious transmutation of one material or property (a lesser valuable substance) to another (a more valuable substance). Mainly, here, I imagine it to mean the physical body transforming into the spirit.

Birds – I used birds to represent two strata of spirits: fowl of the heavens and fowl of the skies. Angels are a fowl of the heavens; these I paired with hawks. I gave crows and vultures the opposite. I believe that W. B. Yeats' "The Second Coming" uses carrion crows as the demonic host that accompany the anti-Christ; they are the "indignant desert birds" reeling about the Sphinx.

Cold and Darkness – The inverse of light and fire; this is negative, a forsaken place of powerlessness and vulnerability.

Compass/Clocks – Time and Place. Help us organize and set a course. As metaphors, these indicate our direction in life, busying oneself wisely and productively. Also, they spin (see Spinning/Turning/Cycles).

Deserts – Suffering is the proof of our existence. I symbolize this suffering with deserts. A desert is a form of "the wilderness" where ogres, traps, and dangers lurk. Each difficulty is its own desert. Also, the mystics retreated to the desert to commune with God. Consider, too, that in a story, the "protagonist" is "the one in agony," from the Greek *Agon*. The narrative arc, here, illustrates a character traversing many agonies.

Dreams – Dreams go where reason cannot. Myths often use dreams to access the special world. So, I use dreams to function as both a portal into and a version of "the wilderness."

Elves – We are not alone. Their physical and magical connections to the stereotypical alien are undeniable.

Fire and Light – God appears as fire. Fire is what Prometheus gave man so that we could be as gods ourselves. Light is knowledge, the presence of God, safety, etc.

Hallucinogens – And here, I plead the 5th. But I had an anonymous friend once who did all kinds of them, and on Brian's advice, I added hints of them throughout the collection.

Heartbreak – I did have my heart broken here. No worries, though. It's gone now, so all's well. Thank you for asking.

Ever making lemonade of my life full of lemons, I used the pain as an inciting incident. Then I built the narrative around abusing pharmaceuticals to cope with it while communing with clockwork elves in DMT's hypergeometric realm of fanning chrysanthemums.

Insects – Most of these insects are the insects of poverty. They are common. Let's say a beloved poet we all know has passed out on a floor; he could encounter one of the insects, which will probably bite him more often than they speak.

Lizards – These are stoics who reject comforts, stripped to subsistence only, existing with nothing between them and God.

Metamorphosis – In my poetry I have grub worms metamorphosizing into elves and dwarves (this comes from Norse Mythology), and since grubs are white, I describe the "pallid husk" as the mortal shell of my character's body. In other poems, I have moths and butterflies-- commonly symbols of metamorphosis. In this collection, metamorphosis relates to such themes as growth, healing, and moving from body to spirit. Transformation takes many forms.

Mirages – Mirages shimmer out of reach. In this collection, they are what we wish for but cannot have.

Moon – In literature, the moon is commonly defined as feminine energy, contrasting the sun's masculine energy. Artemis is much more interesting to me than Selene, so I chose to associate it with her. She is a sister to Apollo. She, too, has a bow and arrows. The Cyclops made her silver bow (being one-eyed, as the moon is one-eyed, with silver light). One of her lesser-known titles is Goddess of Wild Creatures. And though she is usually hostile towards men, I imagined that as my character traverses the desert, she considers him a wild creature, earning her sympathy and compassion.

Opal – Considered a symbol for love, justice, harmony, and passion. It is a protective talisman in dangerous places.

Pills – These are sleeping pills. Sleep is where we dream. So, I use drugs as a catalyst between the known and the unknown (or special) world.

Roses – These emit the breath of God. They are red like heat and passion. God appears as fire. I consider passion relative to heat, so I make the rose analogous to an aspect of God. The dual natures of God and the rose also worked for me. For example, each are beautiful, but if one is careless, he will know the thorn's correction.

Rubies and Diamonds – After W.B. Yeats' "After the Rose," I re-intrepret these two stones, rationalzing that God appears as fire, and rubies appear to have fire trapped within. So, I contrasted them with diamonds, imagining that diamonds are empty and steal the fire they seem to have. Thus, they are imposters, a fool's gold of the burning bush.

Spinning/Turning/Cycles – This is the great mill of the heavens; this is the zodiac, fate, our cycle of life; this is the gyre of the mythos.

Son/Sun – I admit, it is a tired pun, but I could not pass it up. Christians worship Christ, who is "the light" and "the way." Ancients worshiped the sun. God appears as fire. So, as trite as many readers may feel it is, it would have been awkward to ignore. So, join me as I embraced the hell out of it.

Tokens – Charon takes his fee to bring spirits to the other side. I had my character find two coins. These did not come from his own eyes, so he is not dead. However, he interacts with them. He could be close.

Tower – If the Tower of Babel was a monument of man's arrogance, the tower in "A Locust Sings of Armegeddon" is its opposite. God inspired its construction as an earthly symbol of man's brief purity. Because purity in men cannot remain long, God ordered it constructed upon the sand. Purity evaporates in the Deserts of Tribulation, so the tower leans. Its base has further weakened by being tunneled out in various directions so that trains could pass through it. It was a mammoth and magnificent tower. No longer.

Suffering from neglect and abuse, it is in danger of falling. Once it falls, Atlas (the exhausted titan who holds the earth) will adjust the world upon his shoulders for a better grip; this will trigger cataclysmic destruction for mankind.

Trains – Trains are society. Consider that those of us living in society have little to no agency to control it, overall. The individual does not drive it; they cannot stop or turn it left or right, or back it up as it suits them. It is a "public transportation." An exercise of the public will. And though we may move freely aboard its many cars, enter, and exit at intervals of our choosing, we are prisoners of its cohesion.

Troglodyte – His eyes are rubies. He seems to be the second coming of the messiah, but it is a lie. This imposter is not the lizard he, at first, pretends to be. He is as false and greedy of an idol as those which surround him. His eyes are diamonds. He is more serpent than lizard. Though they share initial similarities, they are not the same.

Unusual Vocabulary – Literature (as the ubiquitous "they" say) uses elevated language and explores aspects of the human condition. I would love to claim that my pursuit of creating fine literature made me do it. But I chose those strange words for simpler reasons. I thought they lent the work an unusual and archaic feel. To me, they merely fit the collection's weird subjects. Besides, words are fun! So quitcherbitcin, and look them up if you need to!

Made in the USA
Coppell, TX
07 October 2022

84255460R00062